Mental Maths Practice Ages 5–7

Revision & Practice

KS1 Years 1–2

Build confidence with targeted skills practice

SCHOLASTIC

Published in the UK by Scholastic, 2024

Scholastic Distribution Centre, Bosworth Avenue, Tournament Fields, Warwick, CV34 6UQ

Scholastic Ireland, 89E Lagan Road, Dublin Industrial Estate, Glasnevin, Dublin, D I I HP5F

SCHOLASTIC and associated logos are trademarks and/or registered trademarks of Scholastic Inc.

A catalogue record for this book is available from the British Library.

ISBN 978-0702-32686-8
Printed and bound by Ashford Colour Press

The book is made of materials from well-managed, FSC®-certified forests and other controlled sources.

Author

Paul Hollin

Editorial team

Rachel Morgan, Vicki Yates, Sarah Chappelow, Julia Roberts, David and Jackie Link

Design team

Dipa Mistry and PDQ Media

Illustrations

Tim Bradford/IllustrationX

Contents

How to Use this Book................................4

Addition and Subtraction to 10................6

Addition and Subtraction to 20................8

One More, One Less................................10

Bridging..12

Addition and Subtraction to 100............14

Using Addition......................................16

Using Subtraction..................................18

Multiplication..20

Division..22

Twos, Fives and Tens..............................24

Using Multiplication..............................26

Using Division..28

Answers..30

Progress Tracker....................................32

How to Use this Book

Introduction

This book has been written to help boost the mental maths skills your child has been learning at school. It is designed to reinforce the core mathematical principles to allow quick recall, which will be invaluable as they progress. Although the emphasis of this book is on mental maths, some jottings to aid thinking are fine.

Topic title

Each page starts with a **Recap** of relevant background knowledge your child should already know.

The key content for the area is covered in the **Learn** section. There are clear explanations and examples, using illustrations and diagrams where relevant.

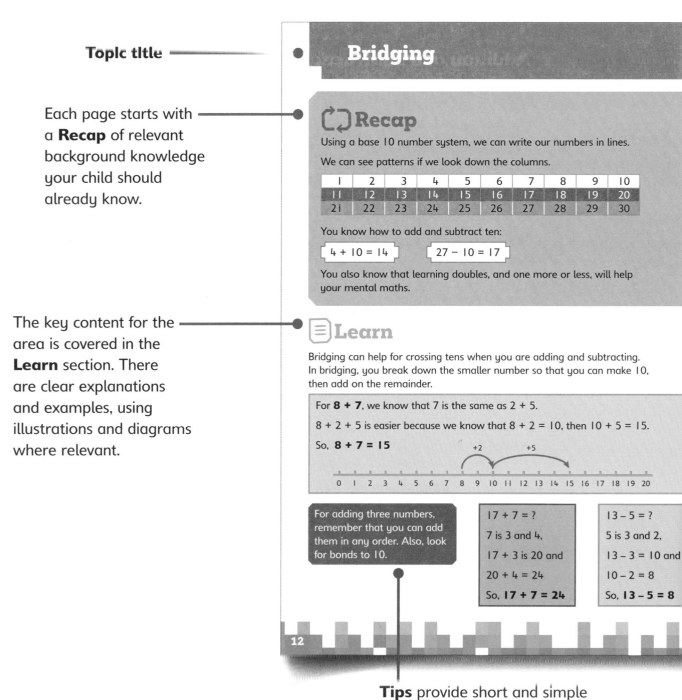

Bridging

⟳ Recap

Using a base 10 number system, we can write our numbers in lines.

We can see patterns if we look down the columns.

1	2	3	4	5	6	7	8	9	10
11	12	13	14	15	16	17	18	19	20
21	22	23	24	25	26	27	28	29	30

You know how to add and subtract ten:

$4 + 10 = 14$ $27 - 10 = 17$

You also know that learning doubles, and one more or less, will help your mental maths.

▤ Learn

Bridging can help for crossing tens when you are adding and subtracting. In bridging, you break down the smaller number so that you can make 10, then add on the remainder.

For **8 + 7**, we know that 7 is the same as 2 + 5.

$8 + 2 + 5$ is easier because we know that $8 + 2 = 10$, then $10 + 5 = 15$.

So, **8 + 7 = 15**

+2   +5

0 1 2 3 4 5 6 7 8 9 10 11 12 13 14 15 16 17 18 19 20

For adding three numbers, remember that you can add them in any order. Also, look for bonds to 10.

$17 + 7 = ?$

7 is 3 and 4,

$17 + 3$ is 20 and

$20 + 4 = 24$

So, **17 + 7 = 24**

$13 - 5 = ?$

5 is 3 and 2,

$13 - 3 = 10$ and

$10 - 2 = 8$

So, **13 − 5 = 8**

Tips provide short and simple advice to aid understanding.

Practice ●───────────────────────── **Practice** a focused range
of questions, with answers

Use bridging on the number line to answer these additions.

a. 7 + 6

| 0 | 1 | 2 | 3 | 4 | 5 | 6 | 7 | 8 | 9 | 10 | 11 | 12 | 13 | 14 | 15 |

_____

at the back of the book.
To check progress and give
practice in what they've
learned.

b. 9 + 6

| 0 | 1 | 2 | 3 | 4 | 5 | 6 | 7 | 8 | 9 | 10 | 11 | 12 | 13 | 14 | 15 |

_____

c. 7 + 9

| 5 | 6 | 7 | 8 | 9 | 10 | 11 | 12 | 13 | 14 | 15 | 16 | 17 | 18 | 19 | 20 |

_____

Show how bridging is used to add these numbers.

a. 7 + 4 = __7__ + __3__ + __1__ = __11__

b. 8 + 5 = _____ + _____ + _____ = _____

c. 4 + 9 = _____ = _____

d. 19 + 4 = _____ = _____

Show how bridging is used to subtract these numbers.

a. 13 – 5 = __13__ – __3__ – __2__ = __8__

b. 12 – 4 = _____ – _____ – _____ = _____

c. 13 – 8 = _____ = _____

d. 19 – 12 = _____ = _____

Addition and Subtraction to 10

 **Recap**

There are 10 digits that we use to make all our numbers:

0	1	2	3	4	5	6	7	8	9
zero	one	two	three	four	five	six	seven	eight	nine

We use numbers to represent groups of objects.

 **Learn**

To add and subtract numbers up to 10 we need to know our number bonds.

We can add 2 groups of objects together.

If we have 5 cubes and 2 cubes, we have 7 cubes altogether.

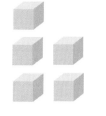

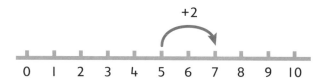

We say 5 add 2 equals 7   5 + 2 = 7

We can take away too. Here are 5 birds.

If 3 birds fly away there will be 2 birds left.

We say 5 minus 3 equals 2   5 − 3 = 2

Practice

1. Find 1 more.

    a. 1 + 1 = _____

    b. 3 + 1 = _____

    c. 4 + 1 = _____

    d. 7 + 1 = _____

    e. 2 + 1 = _____

    f. 9 + 1 = _____

2. Find 1 less.

    a. 4 – 1 = _____

    b. 3 – 1 = _____

    c. 8 – 1 = _____

    d. 9 – 1 = _____

    e. 1 – 1 = _____

    f. 10 – 1 = _____

3. Use the number line to add.

    a. 2 + 3 = _____

    b. 3 + 2 = _____

    c. 4 + 1 = _____

    d. 1 + 4 = _____

    e. 9 + 1 = _____

    f. 1 + 9 = _____

> Remember, the same 3 numbers can be in 4 calculations.
> 4 + 3 = 7   3 + 4 = 7   7 – 4 = 3   7 – 3 = 4

4. Use the number line to subtract.

    a. 5 – 2 = _____

    b. 5 – 3 = _____

    c. 5 – 1 = _____

    d. 5 – 4 = _____

    e. 10 – 9 = _____

    f. 10 – 1 = _____

5. Complete the number sentences.

    a. 5 – 1 = _____

    b. 5 + 2 = _____

    c. 2 + 5 = _____

    d. 7 – 2 = _____

    e. 7 – 5 = _____

    f. 2 + 7 = _____

    g. 9 – 2 = _____

    h. 4 + _____ = 8

    i. 6 – _____ = 2

Addition and Subtraction to 20

⟳ Recap

We have a base 10 number system, which lets us use the digits 0 to 9 to show any amount.

There are 12 birds in the picture.
We show this as 1 ten and 2 ones.

T	O
1	2

This helps with adding above 10:

2 + 3 = 5, so 12 + 3 = 15

5 + 4 = 9, so 5 + 14 = 19

🗐 Learn

Learning the number bonds to 20 will help your mental maths.
Here are some tips:

● Use the bonds to 10 for adding larger numbers.

3 + 2 = 5
so 13 + 2 = 15

6 + 4 = 10
so 16 + 4 = 20

● Learn doubles by heart, such as 2 + 2 = 4 and 7 + 7 = 14.
Use doubles to make other mental additions easier.

8 + 7 = 15
7 + 7 = 14, so 8 + 7 must be 15

● For subtracting smaller numbers, just subtract the ones.

17 − 4 = 13
7 − 4 = 3 and the ten stays the same.

Practice

1. Add and subtract 10.

a. $3 + 10 =$ _____

b. $6 + 10 =$ _____

c. $10 + 2 =$ _____

d. $10 + 0 =$ _____

e. $15 - 10 =$ _____

f. $14 - 10 =$ _____

2. Complete the number bonds to 20.

a. $11 + 9 =$ _____

b. $8 + 12 =$ _____

c. $15 + 5 =$ _____

d. $19 +$ _____ $= 20$

e. $18 +$ _____ $= 20$

f. $16 +$ _____ $= 20$

g. _____ $+ 3 = 20$

h. _____ $+ 13 = 20$

i. _____ $+ 14 = 20$

3. Write the doubles.

a. $1 + 1 =$ _____

b. $2 + 2 =$ _____

c. $3 + 3 =$ _____

d. $4 + 4 =$ _____

e. $5 + 5 =$ _____

f. $6 + 6 =$ _____

g. $7 + 7 =$ _____

h. $8 + 8 =$ _____

i. $9 + 9 =$ _____

4. Add these numbers.

a. $2 + 3 =$ _____

b. $4 + 5 =$ _____

c. $7 + 8 =$ _____

d. $9 + 8 =$ _____

e. $5 + 6 =$ _____

f. $10 + 9 =$ _____

g. $1 + 2 =$ _____

h. $7 + 6 =$ _____

i. $3 + 4 =$ _____

5. Try these subtractions.

a. $15 - 3 =$ _____

b. $9 - 5 =$ _____

c. $15 - 7 =$ _____

d. $17 - 8 =$ _____

e. $7 - 5 =$ _____

f. $19 - 10 =$ _____

g. $2 - 1 =$ _____

h. $13 - 6 =$ _____

i. $16 - 9 =$ _____

6. Find the missing numbers.

a. $2 +$ _____ $= 3$

b. $4 + 7 =$ _____

c. _____ $+ 8 = 10$

d. $13 - 2 =$ _____

e. $5 +$ _____ $= 13$

f. $17 - 9 =$ _____

One More, One Less

 Recap

We can add and subtract 10 using our base 10 number system.

| 10 + 3 = 13 | | 17 − 10 = 7 | | 12 − 10 = 2 |

We know how to add and subtract 1:

| 1 + 3 = 4 | | 17 − 1 = 16 | | 12 − 1 = 11 |

Pick a number and say the numbers next to it. Those numbers are 1 more and 1 less than your starting number.

15 is one more than **14**, and one less than **16**.

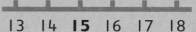

13   14   **15**   16   17   18

 Learn

This mental method is great for improving your addition.

To add 11, add 10 then add 1.
7 + 11 = 18
7 + 10 is 17, **one more** makes 18
4 + 11 = 15
4 + 10 is 14, **one more** makes 15

To add 9, add 10 then subtract 1.
7 + 9 = 16
7 + 10 is 17, **one less** is 16
4 + 9 = 13
4 + 10 is 14, **one less** is 13

We can do the same for subtraction.

To subtract 11, subtract 10 then subtract 1.
13 − 11 = 2
13 − 10 is 3, **one less** is 2
18 − 11 = 7
18 − 10 is 8, **one less** is 7

To subtract 9, subtract 10 then add 1.
13 − 9 = 4
13 − 10 is 3, **one more** is 4
18 − 9 = 9
18 − 10 is 8, **one more** is 9

 **Practice**

1. **Draw lines to connect each number to its addition.**

| 13 | 14 | 15 | 16 | 17 | 18 |

| 7 + 9 | 2 + 11 | 4 + 11 | 9 + 9 | 3 + 11 | 8 + 9 |

2. **Explain how to do each calculation using one more or one less.**

a. 3 + 11 $\underline{\text{3 + 10 makes 13 and one more is 14}}$

b. 6 + 11 _____

c. 6 + 9 _____

d. 15 – 11 _____

e. 15 – 9 _____

3. **Draw lines to connect each number to its subtraction.**

| 2 | 3 | 4 | 5 | 6 | 7 |

| 14 – 11 | 16 – 9 | 14 – 9 | 13 – 11 | 15 – 9 | 15 – 11 |

4. **Answer these additions and subtractions.**

a. 4 + 11 = _____   b. 7 + 11 = _____   c. 11 + 8 = _____

d. 16 – 9 = _____   e. 12 – 11 = _____   f. 17 – 11 = _____

Bridging

↻ Recap

Using a base 10 number system, we can write our numbers in lines.

We can see patterns if we look down the columns.

1	2	3	4	5	6	7	8	9	10
11	12	13	14	15	16	17	18	19	20
21	22	23	24	25	26	27	28	29	30

You know how to add and subtract ten:

$$4 + 10 = 14$$ $$27 - 10 = 17$$

You also know that learning doubles, and one more or less, will help your mental maths.

▤ Learn

Bridging can help for crossing tens when you are adding and subtracting. In bridging, you break down the smaller number so that you can make 10, then add on the remainder.

For **8 + 7**, we know that 7 is the same as 2 + 5.

8 + 2 + 5 is easier because we know that 8 + 2 = 10, then 10 + 5 = 15.

So, **8 + 7 = 15**

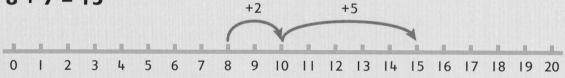

For adding three numbers, remember that you can add them in any order. Also, look for bonds to 10.

17 + 7 = ?

7 is 3 and 4,

17 + 3 is 20 and

20 + 4 = 24

So, **17 + 7 = 24**

13 − 5 = ?

5 is 3 and 2,

13 − 3 = 10 and

10 − 2 = 8

So, **13 − 5 = 8**

Practice

1. **Use bridging on the number line to answer these additions.**

a. 7 + 6

0 1 2 3 4 5 6 7 8 9 10 11 12 13 14 15

_____

b. 9 + 6

0 1 2 3 4 5 6 7 8 9 10 11 12 13 14 15

_____

c. 7 + 9

5 6 7 8 9 10 11 12 13 14 15 16 17 18 19 20

_____

2. **Show how bridging is used to add these numbers.**

a. 7 + 4 = __7__ + __3__ + __1__ = __11__

b. 8 + 5 = _____ + _____ + _____ = _____

c. 4 + 9 = _____ = _____

d. 19 + 4 = _____ = _____

3. **Show how bridging is used to subtract these numbers.**

a. 13 – 5 = __13__ – __3__ – __2__ = __8__

b. 12 – 4 = _____ – _____ – _____ = _____

c. 13 – 8 = _____ = _____

d. 19 – 12 = _____ = _____

Addition and Subtraction to 100

↻ Recap

Knowing your number bonds to 20 is important when you cross over 10.

We can use:

☑ one more, one less:
| 5 + 11 is 5 + 10 + 1 = 16 |

☑ bridging:
| 7 + 5 is 7 + 3 + 2 = 12 |

☑ adding in any order:
| 5 + 7 = 12 and 7 + 5 = 12 |

These methods can help with larger numbers too.

| 33 – 4 = 29 | | 37 + 5 = 42 | | 94 – 9 = 85 |

▤ Learn

Partitioning can help with adding and subtracting 2 large numbers.

In partitioning, we break down each number into its tens and ones, like we would on an abacus.

Partitioning works for subtraction too, but you have to be careful.

Let's try **43 + 25**

4 tens and 2 tens make **6 tens**, or 60

3 ones and 5 ones make **8 ones**

+

6 tens and **8 ones** make 68

T O   T O   T O

4   3   2   5   6   8

| 46 – 12 = 34 | isn't so hard. Using partitioning, we get 3 tens and 4 ones.

But | 43 – 14 = 29 | is harder because the ones in 14 are bigger than the ones in 43.

| 43 – 10 = 33 |, then use bridging | 33 – 3 = 30 | | 30 – 1 = 29 |

Practice

1. Write these additions.

a.

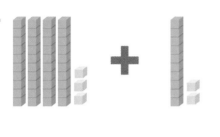

_____ + _____ = _____

b.

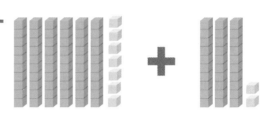

_____ + _____ = _____

2. Do these subtractions using number lines to help you.

a.

25 26 27 28 29 30 31 32 33 34 35 36 37 38 39 40

36 – 8 = _____

b.

10 11 12 13 14 15 16 17 18 19 20 21 22 23 24 25 26 27 28 29 30 31 32 33 34 35

34 – 20 = _____

c.

80 81 82 83 84 85 86 87 88 89 90 91 92 93 94 95 96 97 98 99 100

100 – 18 = _____

3. Now try these calculations.

a. 8 + 4 = _____ **b.** 18 – 4 = _____ **c.** 78 + 4 = _____

d. 23 + 15 = _____ **e.** 35 + 15 = _____ **f.** 69 – 15 = _____

4. Write the missing numbers.

a. 46 + _____ = 57 **b.** 91 – _____ = 86 **c.** 35 + _____ 71

d. 47 – _____ = 27 **e.** 85 – _____ = 70 **f.** _____ + 37 = 82

Using Addition

⟳ Recap

Here are some facts and methods for mental addition:

- Number bonds up to 10
- Number bonds up to 20
- One more, one less

- Partitioning
- Adding 10s
- Bridging

If you aren't sure about any of these, look back through this book.

📄 Learn

We use maths every day, especially for money and measures.
We can use the same mental methods for adding these.

Money: We use **p** to show pence.

$6p + 3p = 9p$

$46p + 15p = 61p$

Weight: We use **g** to show grams.

$8g + 3g = 11g$

$64g + 31g = 95g$

Length: We use **cm** to show centimetres.

$5cm + 7cm = 12cm$

$75cm + 6cm = 81cm$

Capacity: We use **ml** to show millilitres.

$13ml + 7ml = 20ml$

$38ml + 13ml = 51ml$

 **Practice**

1. Add these amounts of money.

    a. 5p + 3p = _____p   b. 8p + 4p = _____p   c. 3p + 2p + 4p = _____p

    d. 12p + 13p = _____p   e. 17p + 9p = _____p   f. 46p + 25p = _____p

2. Add these lengths.

    a. 7cm + 1cm = _____cm   b. 13cm + 12cm = _____cm

    c. 77cm + 20cm = _____cm   d. 37cm + 24cm = _____cm

3. Add these weights.

    a. 12g + 3g = _____g   b. 14g + 6g = _____g   c. 15g + 15g = _____g

    d. 52g + 13g = _____g   e. 59g + 7g = _____g   f. 41g + 35g = _____g

4. Add these capacities.

    a. 7ml + 0ml = _____ml   b. 14ml + 5ml = _____ml

    c. 24ml + 7ml = _____ml   d. 77ml + 16ml = _____ml

5. Find the missing numbers.

    a. 4p + _____p = 9p   b. _____cm + 7cm = 10cm

    c. 16g + _____g = 21g   d. _____ml + 33ml = 44ml

    e. 47p + _____p = 61p   f. _____g + 31g = 60g

    g. 55ml + _____ml = 82ml   h. _____cm + 33cm = 66cm

Using Subtraction

Recap

We can also practise subtraction using measures.

Money: | 6p – 3p = 3p | | 46p – 11p = 35p |

Weight: | 18g – 3g = 15g | | 64g – 31g = 33g |

Length: | 7cm   7cm = 0cm | | 75cm – 6cm = 69cm |

Capacity: | 13ml – 4ml = 9ml | | 57ml – 45ml = 12ml |

 **Learn**

You can improve your mental subtraction if you understand an important fact: **subtraction is the inverse (opposite) of addition.**

We know that if (6 + 7 = 13) then (7 + 6 = 13)

Using inverses we also know that (13 – 6 = 7) and (13 – 7 = 6)

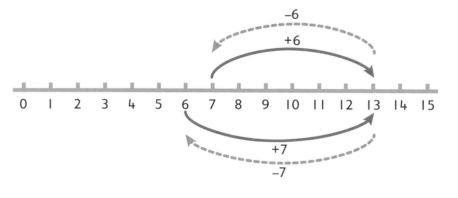

You can practise this by choosing any addition to 20, then thinking of its inverses.

15 + 4 = 19

So, 19 – 15 = 4
and 19 – 4 = 15

 **Practice**

1. **Draw lines to match each subtraction to its answer.**

| 11 | 12 | 13 | 14 | 15 |

| 18 – 5 | 28 – 13 | 34 – 22 | 31 – 20 | 30 – 16 |

2. **Subtract these amounts of money.**

a. 8p – 1p = _____p

b. 9p – 4p = _____p

c. 27p – 9p = _____p

d. 86p – 21p = _____p

3. **Subtract these lengths.**

a. 5cm – 3cm = _____cm

b. 14cm – 10cm = _____cm

c. 43cm – 11cm = _____cm

d. 31cm – 22cm = _____cm

4. **Subtract these weights.**

a. 12g – 9g = _____g

b. 23g – 11g = _____g

c. 79g – 77g = _____g

d. 43g – 25g = _____g

5. **Subtract these capacities.**

a. 5ml – 5ml = _____ml

b. 24ml – 20ml = _____ml

c. 14ml – 9ml = _____ml

d. 90ml – 25ml = _____ml

6. **Find the missing numbers.**

a. 9p – _____p = 2p

b. _____cm – 5cm = 10cm

c. 50g – _____g = 29g

d. _____ml – 33ml = 7ml

Multiplication

 Recap

We can add numbers to find how many we have altogether.

There are 3 pairs of cubes above. Adding the pairs gives 6 cubes altogether.

2 + 2 + 2 = 6

We can also say 3 lots of 2 makes 6, or 3 times 2 equals 6.

 Learn

There are 6 dots.

This pattern of dots is called an array.

Arrays help us group objects and understand multiplication. Above there are three groups of two cubes so the array has two rows of three.

We can say all of these things about the array above:

3 lots of 2 is 6.

3 times 2 is 6.

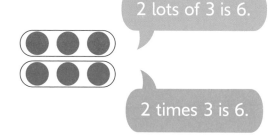

2 lots of 3 is 6.

2 times 3 is 6.

If we had 5 pairs of cubes we could say   2 + 2 + 2 + 2 + 2 = 10

We can count in twos and say that 5 lots of 2 makes 10.

Or we can write $5 \times 2 = 10$

Multiplication is the same as repeated addition.

 **Practice**

1. **Write the calculation that each array shows.**

a. 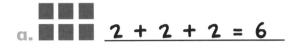 $2 + 2 + 2 = 6$

b.  _____

2. **Shade the dots to make an array for each calculation.**

a. $4 × 2$

b. $2 × 2$

c. $5 × 2$

d. $4 × 5$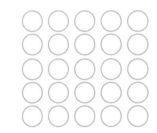

3. **Draw a line from each calculation to its answer on the number line.**

$3 × 2$ $2 × 2$ $10 × 2$ $5 × 2$ $7 × 2$

0 1 2 3 4 5 6 7 8 9 10 11 12 13 14 15 16 17 18 19 20

4. **Write a sentence and a multiplication for each of these additions.**

a. $10 + 10$ two lots of ten makes twenty $2 × 10 = 20$

b. $2 + 2 + 2$ _____   _____

c. $5 + 5 + 5 + 5$ _____   _____

5. **Write the missing numbers.**

a. $3 × 2 =$ _____   b. $5 × 2 =$ _____   c. _____ $× 5 = 10$

Division

 Recap

Multiplication is like repeated addition.

| 2 + 2 + 2 = 6 | 3 lots of 2 makes 6 | 3 × 2 = 6 |

 Learn

If 6 biscuits are shared equally by 2 friends, they will have 3 biscuits each.

> 6 shared between 2 is 3 each.
>
> 6 divided by 2 equals 3.
>
> 6 ÷ 2 = 3

Look at the array below. There are 8 dots altogether.

> 8 shared between 2 is 4 each.
>
> 8 divided by 2 equals 4.
>
> 8 ÷ 2 = 4

Look at the array on the right and these calculations:

| 5 × 2 = 10 | 10 ÷ 2 = 5 |

Both calculations use the same numbers.

Let's look at them on a number line:

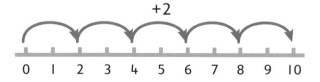

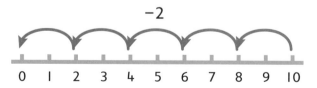

Count 5 steps of 2 from 0 to 10.

5 × 2 = 10

Count back 5 steps of 2 from 10 to 0.

10 ÷ 2 = 5

Practice

1. **Draw lines around half of the objects to share them into 2 equal lots.**
   Write how many are in each lot.

a. 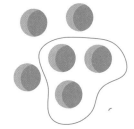   __3__

b. 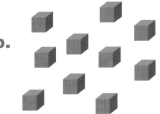   ____

c.    ____

d.    ____

2. **Draw a line round some of the dots to share by 2.**
   Write a calculation next to it.

a.   6 shared by 2 makes 3 $6 \div 2 = 3$

b.   _____   _____

3. **Use the number line to help answer these questions.**

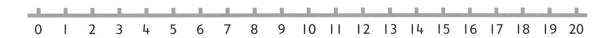

0 1 2 3 4 5 6 7 8 9 10 11 12 13 14 15 16 17 18 19 20

a. $8 \div 2 =$ _____

b. $14 \div 2 =$ _____

c. $18 \div 2 =$

d. $10 \div 5 =$ _____

e. $20 \div 2 -$ _____

f. $15 \div 5 -$ _____

Recap

We know that multiplication is repeated addition, and we know that division is sharing equally.

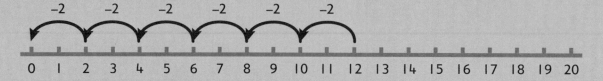

Counting back from 12 to 0 in twos gives us 6. $12 \div 2 = 6$

Learn

This is a multiplication grid and you can use it to find answers to multiplications.

Find the first number in the row at the top and the second number in the column to the side, and where they meet is the answer to your question.

×	0	1	2	3	4	5	6	7	8	9	10	11	12
2	0	2	4	6	8	10	12	14	16	18	20	22	24
5	0	5	10	15	20	25	30	35	40	45	50	55	60
10	0	10	20	30	40	50	60	70	80	90	100	110	120

Can you see that $7 \times 5 = 35$, or that $6 \times 10 = 60$?

Multiplication and division are inverses, so we can use the times tables grid to find answers for both of them.

For example, if we can see that $7 \times 5 = 35$, we also know that $35 \div 5 = 7$

BEWARE! Multiplications can be done in any order, but divisions cannot!

$4 \times 2 = 8$ and $2 \times 4 = 8$

$8 \div 2 = 4$ but $2 \div 8$ **DOES NOT** $= 4$

 **Practice**

1. **Draw lines to match each multiplication to its inverse division.**

| 8 × 5 = 40 | 3 × 10 = 30 | 7 × 2 = 14 | 3 × 5 = 15 |

| 14 ÷ 2 = 7 | 40 ÷ 5 = 8 | 15 ÷ 5 = 3 | 30 ÷ 10 = 3 |

2. **Use the multiplication square on the opposite page to answer each multiplication.**

   a. 6 × 5 = _____   b. 3 × 5 = _____   c. 9 × 5 = _____

   d. 7 × 10 = _____   e. 10 × 10 = _____   f. 5 × 10 = _____

3. **Use the multiplication square to answer each division.**

   a. 40 ÷ 5 = _____   b. 15 ÷ 5 = _____   c. 45 ÷ 5 = _____

   d. 70 ÷ 10 = _____   e. 100 ÷ 10 = _____   f. 50 ÷ 10 = _____

4. **Write three multiplications and three divisions that all have the answer ten.**

   _____ × 2   _____ ÷ 2

   _____ × 5   **10**   _____ ÷ 5

   _____ × 10   _____ ÷ 10

5. **A teacher has 40 biscuits. How many would each child get if she shared them equally with...**

   a. 10 children? _____ biscuits   b. 5 children? _____ biscuits

   c. 2 children? _____ biscuits

Using Multiplication

⟳ Recap

For good mental multiplication you need to know some facts and methods:

- ☑ Multiplication is repeated addition.
- ☑ Multiplication and division are inverses.
- ☑ Two numbers can be multiplied in any order.
- ☑ Know your 2-, 5- and 10-times tables.
- ☑ Arrays can help with multiplication.
- ☑ The 2-times tables give doubles and halves.

If you aren't sure about any of these, look back through this book.

▤ Learn

We can use measures to practise using multiplication in real life.

These examples show different measures being multiplied.

Money: We use **p** to show pence.

| 6 × 2p = 12p | 9 × 10p = 90p |

Weight: We use **g** to show grams.

| 5 × 10g = 50g | 3 × 2g = 6g |

Length: We use **cm** to show centimetres.

| 8 × 5cm = 40cm | double 9cm = 18cm |

Capacity: We use **ml** to show millilitres.

| 4 × 5ml = 20ml | double 8ml = 16ml |

Time: A clock is divided into 5 minute intervals.

| 3 × 5 minutes = 15 minutes | 12 × 5 minutes = 60 minutes (1 hour) |

 **Practice**

1. Find these amounts of money.

   a. 4p × 5 = _____p   b. 8p × 2 = _____p   c. 2p × 5 = _____p

   d. 7 × 10p = _____p   e. 6 × 5p = _____p   f. 3p × 10 = _____p

2. Find these lengths.

   a. 8 × 5cm = _____cm   b. 9 × 2cm = _____cm   c. 4cm × 10 = _____cm

   d. 3cm × 5 = _____cm   e. 8 × 10cm = _____cm   f. 2cm × 10 = _____cm

3. Find these weights.

   a. 5g × 2 = _____g   b. 6 × 10g = _____g   c. 4 × 2g = _____g

   d. 5 × 10g = _____g   e. 3 × 2g = _____g   f. 5g × 5 = _____g

4. Find these capacities.

   a. 9 × 10ml = _____ml   b. 6ml × 2 = _____ml   c. 2ml × 2 = _____ml

   d. 9ml × 5 = _____ml   e. 7ml × 2 = _____ml   f. 1 × 10ml = _____ml

5. Find these times.

   a. 11 × 5 minutes = _____ minutes   b. 3 × 5 minutes = _____ minutes

   c. 10 × 5 minutes = _____ minutes   d. 7 × 5 minutes = _____ minutes

6. Complete each sentence.

   a. If I have six 5p coins, I have _____p altogether.

   b. If I have 12 pencils weighing 10 grams each, they weigh _____ grams altogether.

Using Division

⟲ Recap

Division means dividing a number into equal parts. We also call this sharing.

- We use the symbol ÷ to show division calculations, such a: | 8 ÷ 2 = 4 |

- Multiplication is the inverse of division: | 3 × 5 = 15, so 15 ÷ 5 = 3 |
  This is useful for checking answers.

- We CANNOT divide numbers in any order

  | 6 ÷ 2 = 3, BUT 2 ÷ 6 DOES NOT = 3 |

☰ Learn

These examples show different measures being divided.

Money:

8p shared between 2 people is 4p each.
8p ÷ 2 = 4p

Weight:

10 grams of sugar shared between 2 people
would give 5 grams each. **10g ÷ 2 = 5g**

Length:

6cm can be split into 2 equal
lengths of 3cm. **6cm ÷ 2 = 3cm**

Capacity:

20ml of water can be shared into 5
equal amounts of 4ml. **20ml ÷ 5 = 4ml**

 Practice

1. Divide 20p between different numbers of people.

   a. 20p shared between 2 people: 20p ÷ 2 = _____p each

   b. 20p shared between 5 people: 20p ÷ 5 = _____p each

   c. 20p shared between 10 people: 20p ÷ 10 = _____p each

2. Some pieces of string are cut into equal lengths. Find the lengths.

   a. 12cm divided into 2 lengths: 12cm ÷ 2 = _____cm each

   b. 70cm divided into 10 lengths: 70cm ÷ 10 = _____cm each

   c. 30cm divided into 5 lengths: 30cm ÷ 5 = _____cm each

3. Find these weights.

   a. 25g ÷ 5 = _____g   **b.** 16g ÷ 2 = _____g   **c.** 90g ÷ 10 = _____g

4. Find these capacities.

   a. 16ml ÷ 2 = _____ml **b.** 20ml ÷ 5 = _____ml **c.** 30ml ÷ 10 = _____ml

5. Find these times.

   a. 20 minutes ÷ 2 = _____ minutes   **b.** 45 minutes ÷ 5 = _____ minutes

6. Complete each sentence.

   a. If 2 × 7 = 14, then _____ ÷ _____ = _____, or _____ ÷ _____ = _____

   b. 70p is shared equally between 7 people. They get _____p each.

   c. A jug with 20ml of water can fill _____ cups that hold 5ml each.

   d. I can listen to _____ 3-minute songs in 15 minutes.

Answers

Pages 6–7 Addition and Subtraction to 10

1. a. 2   b. 4   c. 5   d. 8   e. 3   f. 10
2. a. 3   b. 2   c. 7   d. 8   e. 0   f. 9
3. a. 5   b. 5   c. 5   d. 5   e. 10   f. 10
4. a. 3   b. 2   c. 4   d. 1   e. 1   f. 9
5. a. 4   b. 7   c. 7   d. 5   e. 2   f. 9
   g. 7   h. 4   i. 4

Pages 8–9 Addition and Subtraction to 20

1. a. 13   b. 16   c. 12   d. 10   e. 5   f. 4
2. a. 20   b. 20   c. 20   d. 1   e. 2   f. 4
   g. 17   h. 7   i. 6
3. a. 2   b. 4   c. 6   d. 8   e. 10   f. 12
   g. 14   h. 16   i. 18
4. a. 5   b. 9   c. 15   d. 17   e. 11   f. 19
   g. 3   h. 13   i. 7
5. a. 12   b. 4   c. 8   d. 9   e. 2   f. 9
   g. 1   h. 7   i. 7
6. a. 1   b. 11   c. 2   d. 11   e. 8   f. 8

Pages 10–11 One More, One Less

1.

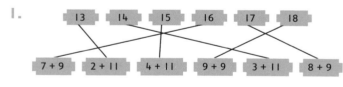

2. b. 6 + 10 makes 16 and one more is 17
   c. 6 + 10 makes 16 and one less is 15
   d. 15 – 10 makes 5 and one less is 4
   e. 15 – 10 makes 5 and one more is 6

3.

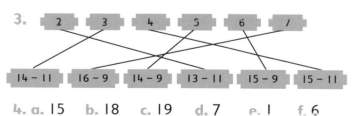

4. a. 15   b. 18   c. 19   d. 7   e. 1   f. 6

Pages 12–13 Bridging

1. a. 13   b. 15   c. 16
2. b. 8 + 2 + 3 = 13
   c. 3 + 1 + 9 = 13 or 4 + 6 + 3 = 13
   d. 19 + 1 + 3 = 23
3. b. 12 – 2 – 2 = 8
   c. 13 – 3 – 5 = 5
   d. 19 – 9 – 3 = 7

Pages 14–15 Addition and Subtraction to 100

1. a. 43 + 12 = 55   b. 67 + 32 = 99
2. a. 28   b. 14   c. 82
3. a. 12   b. 14   c. 82   d. 38   e. 50   f. 54
4. a. 11   b. 5   c. 36   d. 20   e. 15   f. 45

Pages 16–17 Using Addition

1. a. 8p   b. 12p   c. 9p   d. 25p
   e. 26p   f. 71p
2. a. 8cm   b. 25cm   c. 97cm   d. 61cm
3. a. 15g   b. 20g   c. 30g   d. 65g
   e. 66g   f. 76g
4. a. 7ml   b. 19ml   c. 31ml   d. 93ml
5. a. 5p   b. 3cm   c. 5g   d. 11ml
   e. 14p   f. 29g   g. 27ml   h. 33cm

Pages 18–19 Using Subtraction

1.

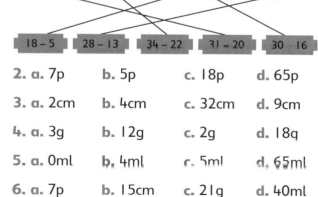

2. a. 7p   b. 5p   c. 18p   d. 65p
3. a. 2cm   b. 4cm   c. 32cm   d. 9cm
4. a. 3g   b. 12g   c. 2g   d. 18g
5. a. 0ml   b. 4ml   c. 5ml   d. 65ml
6. a. 7p   b. 15cm   c. 21g   d. 40ml

Pages 20–21 Multiplication

1. b. 2 + 2 + 2 + 2 = 8

2. a.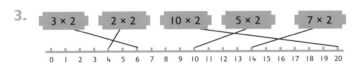
   b.
   c.
   d.

3.

| 3 × 2 | 2 × 2 | 10 × 2 | 5 × 2 | 7 × 2 |

```
0  1  2  3  4  5  6  7  8  9  10  11  12  13  14  15  16  17  18  19  20
```

4. b. three lots of two makes six, 3 × 2 = 6
   c. four lots of five makes twenty, 4 × 5 = 20

5. a. 6   b. 10   c. 2

Pages 22–23 Division

1. b. 5   c. 4   d. 7

2. b. 8 shared by 2 makes 4, 8 ÷ 2 = 4

3. a. 4   b. 7   c. 9   d. 2   e. 10   f. 3

Pages 24–25 Twos, Fives and Tens

1.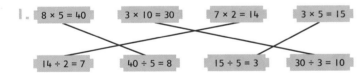

| 8 × 5 = 40 | 3 × 10 = 30 | 7 × 2 = 14 | 3 × 5 = 15 |

| 14 ÷ 2 = 7 | 40 ÷ 5 = 8 | 15 ÷ 5 = 3 | 30 ÷ 3 = 10 |

2. a. 30   b. 15   c. 45   d. 70   e. 100   f. 50

3. a. 8   b. 3   c. 9   d. 7   e. 10   f. 5

4.

5 × 2   20 ÷ 2

2 × 5   **10**   50 ÷ 5

1 × 10   100 ÷ 10

5. a. 4 biscuits   b. 8 biscuits   c. 20 biscuits

Pages 26–27 Using Multiplication

1. a. 20p   b. 16p   c. 10p   d. 70p
   e. 30p   f. 30p

2. a. 40cm   b. 18cm   c. 40cm   d. 15cm
   e. 80cm   f. 20cm

3. a. 10g   b. 60g   c. 8g   d. 50g
   e. 6g   f. 25g

4. a. 90ml   b. 12ml   c. 4ml   d. 45ml
   e. 14ml   f. 10ml

5. a. 55 minutes   b. 15 minutes
   c. 50 minutes   d. 35 minutes

6. a. 30p   b. 120 grams

Pages 28–29 Using Division

1. a. 10p   b. 4p   c. 2p

2. a. 6cm   b. 7cm   c. 6cm

3. a. 5g   b. 8g   c. 9g

4. a. 8ml   b. 4ml   c. 3ml

5. a. 10 minutes   b. 9 minutes

6. a. 14 ÷ 7 = 2, or 14 ÷ 2 = 7
   b. 10p
   c. 6 cups
   d. 5 3-minute songs

Progress Tracker

Practised	Achieved		
☐	☐	**Addition and Subtraction to 10**	6
☐	☐	**Addition and Subtraction to 20**	8
☐	☐	**One More, One Less**	10
☐	☐	**Bridging**	12
☐	☐	**Addition and Subtraction to 100**	14
☐	☐	**Using Addition**	16
☐	☐	**Using Subtraction**	18
☐	☐	**Multiplication**	20
☐	☐	**Division**	22
☐	☐	**Twos, Fives and Tens**	24
☐	☐	**Using Multiplication**	26
☐	☐	**Using Division**	28

Well done!

You have completed the
Mental Maths Practice
book

Name: _____

Date: _____